Jugglers of Light

First published May 2010 by Shalom House Poetry,
31 The Cairn, Newtownabbey, Country Antrim, BT36 6YF.

ISBN :   978-0-9564588-0-3

©Copyright for the poems in this collection remains with Tom Honey
No part of this book may be reproduced or transmitted in any form or by any means without written permission from the publisher, except by a reviewer who wishes to quote brief passages in connection with a review written for insertion in a newspaper, magazine or broadcast. All information contained within the book is correct at the time of going to press.

Printed by Europaprint

Cover design by Michelle and Ross Taylor

for Vivien
with my best wishes
Tom

Jugglers of Light

Tom Honey

Shalom House Poetry

Tom Honey's first collection *A View of Water* was published in December 2005 by Shalom House Poetry. This second collection is published by the same group. He gratefully acknowledges the help given him by many people.

Janice and the late James Simmons and visiting poets at Poets' House

Carol Rumens & Jean Bleakney of the former Friday Group.

The Scribbler Group.

Dr. Edith Newman Devlin for her unfailing encouragement.

This present collection owes much to the help of his colleagues of the Shalom Writers' Group and in particular to Denis O'Sullivan, Secretary/Treasurer, who gave generously of his time to the preparation of the text. Grateful thanks also to the poets Ruth Carr and Moyra Donaldson, tutors to the Group.

Ross and Michelle Taylor designed the cover based on a photograph taken by Michelle of Reilly and Flynn Dennison. Tom gratefully acknowledges their contribution.

He also expresses his deep thanks to Pauline, Peter and all the family for their loving encouragement.

The poems *Haymaking, All of us Children, Winter Flowering Cherry* appeared previously in the anthology *A Trail of Silver Papers* in 2007. *Six Days* was first published in Turning Point in the competition issue of the Creative Writers' magazine in 2007. *A Dearth of Princes* and *Signs of Change* were recorded in Audio Anthologies of 2009 & 2010 respectively, part of New Belfast Community Arts Initiative.

Contents

Honig	9
Goat's Milk	10
Kate 'n Anne	11
Sloak	12
Divestiture	13
Jugglers of Light	14
A Lament for Strings	15
Once on Portavogie Beach	16
A May Meditation	17
High Flier	18
Tuck Shop	19
Living Dangerously	20
A Dearth of Princes	21
A Good Read	22
If Hell Has Music	23
Aurally Challenged	24
The Years	25
Conversations with Conal	26
Journeying	27
Let's Dance	28
Privacy	29
The Window	30
Enlargement	31
Artefact	33
Art and the Cognoscenti	34
Fences and Neighbours	36
Six Days	38
All of us Children	39
Da n d e l i o n s	40
Cheering the Train	41
Early Learning	42
Signs of Change	43
The Heavy Gang	44
Scar	45

Technology	46
Spring Song	47
Greetings	48
Latitudes 1	49
Latitudes 2	50
A Gift from the Night	51
Hello, Mossoró	52
Vendors on the Avenida	53
Memory Burr	54
Water-Lilies	55
Weeds and Wheels	56
H a y m a k i n g	57
Josie	59
Safe House	60
Freety People	61
Attaboy	62
Famine in the Skies	63
Intruder	64
Taking October Slowly	65
Irrelevant	66
Rough Crossing	67
Shots	68
Dodecahedron	69
Value for Money	70
Easy Pleasing	71
School Outing	72
All the Hands	74
The Eleven Plus	75
Still that Face	76
The Lights Gone Dead	77
Praise Him	78
Winter-Flowering Cherry	79

In memory of my parents

Sidney and Ellen Honey

Honig

Seen on a shelf in Lidl the label
on a jar arrested me. *HONIG* it read
and in an instant, late-forties memories
swept over me - family ration books,
long queues, post-war privations.

Otto was the name. Otto Honig
writing from a ruined Germany,
trawling for pen-friends in some list
he'd come across "Our names mean the same."
he wrote to Peter, our family's youngest.

"Please write." then "Please send parcels."
The coffee we disguised in a plain tin,
as he'd instructed. Some biscuits, cheese,
a bar or two of chocolate, boiled sweets
but not much else. Nothing too fragile.

The parcels made their way to Freiburg.
We saved the stamps from his replies.
We still dispute what brought the contact
to an end. Did the novelty wear off?
With vague regrets in mind, I bought a jar.

Goat's Milk

Frail baby, your mother also weak,
it was decided that some country air
and fare might see you through,
your father's mother willing to care for you.

But failing that – your father's practicality –
you'd be a small burden for burial,
the grave-yard only a step along the road.
Granny Conway would have none of it.

She swore by goat's milk. Nothing better
for an ailing child. That, and her care,
brought you back from death's door,
restored to family a bouncing girl.

Thanks to that goat, and granny too,
you lived to see your own grandchildren
and on the way produced the four of us,
guiding us in ways we never came to rue.

Kate 'n Anne

Kate and Anne, sisters hunched with age,
their faces marvellously wrinkled,
like witches almost, but benevolent,
would smile toothlessly when welcoming us.

Their cottage was at the end of a lane
where grasshoppers tick-ticked in
flowery verges, and evenings were
sweet with the fragrance of wild woodbine.

They knew all their cows by name; gave
ducks and chickens the run of the place.
We bought our milk and eggs from them
when summer drew us to the country

"He's goin' to be tall" Kate said one day
to mother. "Big knees", she added, eyeing
mine, showing below my short pants.
Anne smiled "That's how you tell with calves"

I savoured that hope and lived with it
all through adolescence, marking my height
on the wall until one day it dawned:
Kate n' Anne had got things woefully wrong.

Sloak

We, at the senior edge of the family,
salivate at the memory of sloak.
"Sloak? What's that?" people would ask.

As children we enjoyed the incredulous
looks of visitors when a cooked portion
of the seaweed was plopped on our plates

to supplement egg, bacon and taty bread.
"You're not going to eat that, are you" they'd ask.
"It's like something you'd see under a hen roost!"

Our response, after spreading a layer
of the black-green pulp on fried bread,
was to munch it with noisy pleasure..

"It's a lifetime since we stocked it." They said
at Sawers. Like the blue skies of childhood,
seems almost as if we had imagined it.

Divestiture

That ageing male heading into town
in rainbow hued shorts set me
recalling days of navy serge suits,
modest hem lengths, and all those
buttoned-up folk that peopled my youth.
Concession to summer, an open-necked shirt,
ladies would bare their arms.

Roger Casement in Amazonas
seen aboard ship on the Putumayo,
still in Irish tweeds and hat despite
the equatorial sun. For pity's sake!

The sixties untied the winds
that loosened everything. Clothes
were to die and come to life again.
Divestiture was in. Decade of mixed
blessings, setting me on divergent
paths, eager for new ways, but
still trailing old decencies.

Jugglers of Light

Sometimes on sunny days we'd opt
to play the mirrors game, and each
was charged to sneak one from the house.
We'd choose a good position, backs
to a gable wall and scoop the sun,
becoming jugglers of light,
loosing bright streams of squares
and circles along the shady side,
sending them dancing, frail as butterflies,
over the bricks , around doorways
and windows, mingling, quivering,
a restless flood that lifted
the gloom from sunless walls.
To make a change we'd trespass
into homes, halo-ing holy pictures,
highlighting family photos,
which brought indignant rapping
on the window pane. One lady
raged that we were out to blind
her pet canary ! Sure we were
only having fun, we said. Then,
when the sun had had enough of us
it found a cloud, and we turned home,
slipped mirrors back where they belonged.

A Lament for Strings
For Tony Smyth

It took a bit of coaxing but his parents
finally got him a violin; shiny,
beautiful, the colour of new chestnuts.
He carried it now carefully in its case,

avoiding wee girls swinging on the lamp,
and boys playing handball against the gable.
He knew where a music teacher lived. Had often
seen him, always in black, carrying his violin.

Saw him one day enter a house with a polished
brass plaque at the door; a foreign name.
He just knew he could learn from that teacher.
Could hear the strings singing in his head!

Smiled as he imagined himself playing *Ave Maria*
for his mammy. And maybe one day he'd
join a ceilidhe band, play in the Ard Scoil.
Imagine ! A Belfast one like the *Kilfenora!*

He was warm when he reached the teacher's house,
The plaque looked dull today. Had to knock twice.
"What do you want, wee lad?" a woman asked.
He held up his violin. "I want to learn"

"Ach, son, yer too late. My Rudi died last month"
He couldn't think of what to say, as the door closed.
The violin felt heavy now, his sweaty shirt cold.
He turned back down the street, taking the long way home.

Once on Portavogie Beach

Sun in my eyes as I paddled,
I hardly saw the two boys approach.
"Hey, wee lad" They drew closer.
"What are yuh?" The water felt colder.
Their question, I sensed vaguely,
was not to be answered.

I crab-sidled away from them.
Again, louder."Hey, what are yuh?"
Sand was running from between my toes.
"I don't know. I've-I've – no sense"
They responded kicking water round me.

"Who were those boys? my mother asked
when I retreated to the family redoubt
among the beach umbrellas.
I made the most of my story, expecting
plaudits; was stung by their laughter.

A May Meditation

From the CIE bus passengers
alight, tourists from the south.
Cameras come alive, absorbing all
the sun has beautified – warm cheeks
of Belfast Castle, barbered greens,
the fountain drinking light,
the homing ferry glowing as it
parts the waters of the Lough.

But no one ascends the path
to photograph the woods ribboned
in blue. No one catches the scents
of the May morning. They miss
the stillness of the bluebells massed
beneath the trees, heads bent as if
attentive to a distant Angelus.

High Flier

Suddenly, there it was, inches
away from my foot, a stunned bird
cradled on poppy foliage,
its wings' dark sickle spread.
A green frond stirring gently
proved the small heart pulsing still.

A quarter hour I sat unmoving.
This swift, somehow made helpless,
was one subtracted from the numbers
cutting arcs in the evening sky.

I slipped indoors, put through a call
to summon a knowledgeable friend,
but my relief was nearer to disappointment
when we found the bird no longer
anywhere around. We scanned the sky
and hoped our swift was once again
part of that high-flying company
screeching overhead.

Tuck Shop

It was our refreshment stop when,
sweaty from trudging up the road,
we'd spend our ha'pence on a string
of licorice, sweety cigarettes or kali-suckers.
Then, fortified, we'd pass under
the old arches to the foothills and work
our way up towards McArt's Fort
and the adventures promised
by a day on Cavehill.

Even after it had stopped trading
that little shop was a nod to past pleasures.
But time, a sagging roof and rotting
woodwork advertised relentless decay.
"Why do they leave it there?" people wondered.
Then last week it was suddenly yanked
like a troublesome tooth. The gap revealed
a green confusion, but also the bright face
of a white-walled house smiling its relief.

Living Dangerously

The teacher's frantic gestures
and shrill blasts on the whistle
brought us charging back through
hindering waves to the beach.
We gathered round him. "Look" he said.
Our eyes followed his pointing finger.
"Out there.Can you see it? A shark!"
"Shark?" Unbelievingly "Shark?"
And at last, far-off, we saw the fin
cleaving the grey green surface.
"Yes!" We squealed in counterfeit alarm
but hugged ourselves with private joy;
so nearly been victims! Something
monstrous had visited us, sown menace
in the quiet waters of Cushendun Bay.
This was worth writing home about.

"Basking shark" said local fishermen.
"Wouldn't harm a soul" But we would not
be denied our brush with death, even
when a dead one, entangled in nets,
was dragged ashore. We got to touch it.
One man, sensing our need, sliced bits
of skin, sandpaper rough, and passed
them to outstretched, straining hands.
Of course in time the relics stank,
but still were our records of the day
we nearly didn't make it home.

A Dearth of Princes

Old Cavehill Road: a lady's silver shoe
perched on the kerb- rather incongruous
this Monday morning – stirs curiosity,
amused surprise. Size five and almost new
so speculative comments gather pace.
Someone reminds us that the Chester's near
at hand. Could it be just the usual?
Young gadabout, round midnight, helped
to a cab, pushed hastily aboard,
all unaware her shiny pair's now one.
Next morning she will look for it but fail
to recollect too clearly the night before.
As princes hereabouts are rarely seen,
unfriendly even, often on the dole,
the chance of a romantic follow-up
is nil. The shelf-life of a fairy-tale
on this old road, sadly, very brief,
leaving a Cinderella to her grief.

A Good Read

That's what he said he wanted.
Irish flavour, open air. Nothing
demanding. I suggested Maurice Walsh,
then much in favour. And Maurice won him.
The Small Dark Man, While Rivers Run,
Green Rushes, Blackcock's Feather,
many more. Devotion complete,
he got himself fishing gear, a dog,
acquired homespuns and bought
a point two two. City lad, he soon
immersed himself in country ways,
trying the life his heroes seemed to live
in Walsh land. I marvelled how
a "good read" had opened him
to new pursuits. Wondered whether
I had ever been drawn by reading
into action. Recalled only one thing.
Once as a boy, after *Black Beauty* ,
I wandered city streets in search
of a horse, my pocket full of bread.

If Hell Has Music

Like something dying dreadfully
the sound declines as he taps
lightly on the classroom door.
"Good morning, Father. You're just
in time." Miss Pepper smiles.
"A little treat. Bring Father that chair"
The class of boys, recorders raised,
are poised for the assault, but she
creams off the best of them
and rings them round his reverence.
"Ready now. Deep breath- one, two, three"
The musical octet takes off
with *Ten Green Bottles*. The sound,
like wind strangled in a keyhole,
afflicts him. His pasted smile sags
as he silently concludes that
Lenten rigours would be preferable.
The performers pause before
attacking *Old Macdonald*.
His reverence rises rapidly,
applauding energetically.
"Well done, boys. Keep it up.
What talent ! Sorry Miss. Must go"
Excuse is that he's under orders.
Leaves, certain that, if Hell has music,
it must be that of recorders.

Aurally Challenged

His way was to lean forward,
one hand cupping an ear
the better to hear what was said
in church.

And all a fellow could do
when his dad so advertised
a minor disability
was shrink.

More years behind me now
than dad ever had, my ears
are disadvantaged by the way
people speak.

All fail to articulate
distinctly. Even at the mike
their words crumble into
incoherence.

I contain my impatience
while straining to hear them,
certain that a stoical restraint
becomes me.

The Years

*You're looking great.
You haven't changed a bit!*
Some say.

But, years are not fooled.
They have no appetite for cant
and, mustered in decades,
incline to throw their weight around.

They're pressing close these days,
hissing uncomfortable truths,
hints about sticks, zimmers even!
They're clipping my heels,

nipping my hips, dimming my eyes,
giving the odd shove
to make a fellow
lose confidence

So, if by chance we meet,
don't say I'm looking well.
Remember, the years have ears.

Conversations with Conal

Mostly he'd ask about the olden days,
days, that is, when I was the age he is now
and I'd tell him tales of horse-and-cart
deliveries around the streets – the coalman,
black-faced, with heavy loads on his shoulders,
the woman who used to wear a man's cap,
back to front, pushing a barrow, yelling
Ardglass Herrings, drawing the local cats.
The lovely smell from the bread-cart's
open doors revealing shelves of fresh
loaves, scones, barmbracks and tarts.

The stories ripened with repetition.
Once, his curiosity startled me.
"Tell me about the IRA"
I searched the small face, the earnest eyes.
Six, and he wants to know about the RA!
Cautiously I probed "What about them?"
He shifted a little "Just wanna know –
when they go to the loo, do they take off
their masks?" I chose not to laugh,
and, never privy to the ways of subversives,
failed that day to provide enlightenment.

Journeying
For Pauline, Jim and Peter

We drove between high hedges on the road
that still retained its country quietness, almost
as though forgotten by the County board.
The air through the open window was sweet.

She breathed in appreciatively, began to talk.
"Nothing much has changed in all these years
since we walked this way to school each day,
two miles there and back again. " She smiled.

"That mossy bank is where is where we used to pick
wild strawberries. We ate hawthorn leaves,
our bread-and-cheese. And of course blackberries
Sucked primroses and honeysuckle.

The young McLaughlins walked barefoot,
soles tough as leather. Sometimes we'd get a sail
in a farmer's bright, orange cart. The horse
took its time, but we didn't mind!"

She grew quiet. No cars had passed us. No houses
showed along the way. The silence deepened
the sense of remoteness, of time suspended,
our journey more inward than onward.

A distant, muffled rumble reached us, reminding
that a main road lay ahead. We slowed,
dropping down the gears, and edged
toward the junction and the world of wheels.

Let's Dance

The ballet season at the Opera House
had come and gone, but she stayed charmed,
reliving Swan Lake and the dazzle
of Coppelia, opining publicly about

the merits of the Bolshoi and the Kirov
though she knew neither. Said she would
have seen Nureyev and Fonteyn perform
the year before in London but for the queues.

She strutted her own catwalk round the City Hall,
affecting Russian gear; white Cossack hat,
fur collar, calf-length coat of heavy stuff,
and boots. Even her speech waxed balletic,

with scintillating words like pirouettes,
glissades and arabesques. Her looks, I thought,
grew fetchingly more Slav, eyes of an Arctic
chill I fancied, so I asked her to a dance.

Club Orchid, Thursday night. I hoped to melt
her with my tango learned just months before
on Latin evenings, Neely's studio.
But no! A sack of spuds would show

more animation on the dance floor
than my home-grown Muscovite.
I left her to the taxi rank but knew
there'd be no encore of our pas-de-deux.

Privacy

Very private, they said of him.
Never opens to visitors.
To anyone. Keeps himself
to himself.

Talk that he took a sup
was labelled nasty gossip.
A gentleman. Bothers no one.
So polite, refined, they said.

Once from my window I saw him
open his back door,
turn to the sky and howl –
quietly withdraw.

The Window

Grey days do it no favours
but this morning sun is generous,
warming the group of figures,
returning life to the story
chronicled in stained glass.

Viewing that window I marvelled,
the Nativity alight as I had never seen it.
Such a range of blues and purples,
bright golds and aquamarines,
the Holy Family gloriously robed.

These panes must have glowed like this
while in the artist's studio
before time's dross had gathered
through eighty winters.
Why this transfiguration now?

Surely it was my renovated eye
that stripped away dullness, seeing
new loveliness. Tempting, then,
to believe this other-worldly glow
was meant especially for me.

Enlargement

1

The cast of that school concert photographed
decades ago emerged in the enlargement.
Forty eight small boys, half of them in frocks
and bonnets, some looking rather serious.
The little bride, a dream in white!

Amusement as we identified ourselves.
Amazement that we even recalled
the show's song *The Wedding of the Painted Doll*
Our mood sobered as we remembered
those death had taken. Wondered about others.

We spoke about the little groom decked in tails,
black tie, top hat, the bride on his arm.
Noel Fitzpatrick of the choir boy face,
gentle like his brother Raymund
whom he followed into the priesthood

2

Westrock Drive, July 9, 1972

An I.R.A truce had fractured. Ballymurphy,
afflicted by gunfire all that night.
Soldiers sniping from the nearby timber yard,
the people said. A school girl dead.
Fr. Noel , curate at the church, responded.

A parishioner went with him as he left
to give the Last Rites to the dead.
The next shot killed them both, the bullet,
high velocity, passing through each.
Two youths who tried to reach the priest died too.

The Requiem Mass for Fr. Noel drew
dignitaries of all sorts, and the people.
His brother Raymund was chief celebrant.
An Army statement later claimed that soldiers
only targeted those seen bearing arms.

Artefact
i.m. Jim

Look for them in ploughed land,
we'd been told. A field on the Toome road
was where we bent backs to gather flints
and filled our pockets with a load.

One find was special. Small, grey-white,
symmetrical, its slim leaf shape sparked
our imagination. An arrowhead for sure,
its edges delicately chipped and sharp;

surely a weapon lacking just the shaft.
The geology teacher clinched our view
and, fingering the flint admiringly,
suggested that in time we could

donate it to the school's flint hoard.
We were in favour of the plan.
To no avail. I was deprived of it
that day by some, furtive thieving hand.

Of all the objects I have lost to thieves
across a lifetime, no loss cut more
than that small artefact some expert hand
had wrought millennia before.

Art and the Cognoscenti
(Antonio Correggio 1487 – 1534)

With a cruel jibe the canon scoffed at
Correggio's new fresco in the cupola
of Parma's cathedral. It was, he said
A hash of frogs' legs!

The theme was the Assumption of Mary
into heaven, accompanied by angels
and saints, a work of much labour accomplished
on rickety scaffolding in the dome.

But the people loved the grandeur of the theme,
the soft colouring, the flowing draperies
and marvelled at the figures ascending,
drawing all eyes upward to the light.

Some, though, had other thoughts. When Titian
came to Parma they urged him to repaint
the cupola with a subject of his own.
The maestro's expert eye surveyed the fresco.

"Were you to overturn that dome,
and fill it with silver, you would not
compensate the artist for his great work"
With that the critics held their tongue.

    * * * * * *

Five centuries on we watch the building
       of an elevator to the dome meant
for the cognoscenti come to Parma
to acclaim again the artist and his art.

Fences and Neighbours

A bid for privacy,
front-of-the-road necessity
so they planted trees.

Cypresses especially,
making living fences
around their property.

In no time at all, foot
after vertical foot, hand over
hand they reached the roof.

I was soon denied
my familiar skyline
by the evergreen tide.

No view of flowers
breaking through in other gardens
no red roofs or spires.

Yesterday saws sang
through multiple decapitations
and the neighbourhood rang.

From my front door I reclaim
for the first time in years
Cave Hill's caves again.

And old McArt's Fort
taking the morning sun,
is a loved painting restored.

Landscape is redefined
and for a space, it seems,
time is on rewind.

Six Days

Each cloudless morning I gain a matchless view
from here outside the Spar. Thirty miles
or more away- *those blue, remembered hills-*
Slieve Donard, Bernagh, Commedagh all smiles,
plying their quiet seductiveness again.

I resist. I wont leap fifty
Eastertides to replicate that Easter
when six of us, took on the Mournes, heaved
weighty rucks up the Hare's Gap, a tester
for the week ahead. We rhymed the litany

of peaks that ringed our six days hostelling,
days of bladed winds, untrammelled sun
and snow in crevices. We ate for sixty-six,
it seemed, in Bloody Bridge, Knockbarra,
Slievenaman; groaned as our city bones

learned the hard way what trekking cost;
yet we agreed we'd never had such fun,
nor ever did again. Time now to shelve
the memory. Coax these yellowed
contours back into their folds.

All of us Children

A day of swirl and bluster –
wands of mayflower stirring in the hedge
and in the ditch, cow parsley cheering,
fields flickering with streaming grass
and all the trees galloping.
Time, we thought, to give Paul's kite
an airing. So ,with a tail of little paper bows
attached we flung it to the breeze.
It bucked, gyrated, dived
and three times bit the earth.

We improvised with plastic bags,
tethered them with string,
then proffered them in hope.
The wind obliged. To our delight,
all ballooned and scrambled
for the clean-swept sky.
Great gusts enveloped us, and even
coaxed the kite to circle like a hawk.
Caught in the day's tempestuous hug
all of us children – five to fifty five –
gave vent to our exuberance.
Wind-filled, light-filled, wildly prancing,
each one partnered a bag-balloon
and spent the mad hour dancing.

Dandelions
For Edith

No less a host than Wordsworth's daffodils
you shake your gold umbrellas in the sun.
Yes, dandelions, propagate yourselves;
the sight of yellow multitudes can stun.
You know, in spite of humble origins,
that you are fit to colonise the earth.
It's true, sometimes, the garden sprayer wins
But what's a small defeat? You know your worth.

You bloom in spite of rubble at your feet.
You burst through concrete crevices, ignore
the strewn carry-outs, the dirty street
and smile, for you have seen it all before.
You send your wingéd children through the air
and bless them with a dandelion prayer.

Cheering the Train

The curved embankment by the railway lines
gathers the sun; teems with dandelions.
They stand, those thousands, in expectant pose,
as though awaiting a familiar noise.
Soon there's a tremor and a distant hum,
spurring the mood of excitement among
the flowery multitude . Earth resounds
to the chant of the evening train as it rounds
the curve and, just before disappearing,
weathers a storm of soundless cheering.

Early Learning

Ten black pom-poms jostle close to mother,
liking the water world just newly theirs.
But, in a gleam of wings, a sharp-billed gull
sweeps in an arc towards them.
The water bristles. They're instantly gone.
The bird lifts, hovers, waiting
the conjuring trick to be reversed.
The family reappears, prompting another
low pass over them, but water fusses
round the chicks as again they dive.
A third attempt meets with the same
response. The black-back soars and leaves.
Breakfasting resumes,but watchfully.
Early learning for the pom-pom class.

Signs of Change
the Waterworks Revisited

Too early yet for the bulrushes
still in their bleached wretchedness
like the ruins of a blitzed town.
But the sheen on the willow catkins
and the flurry of wings tell better news.
No visitors today to the old raft,
half submerged, where, yesterday,
nine nervy cormorants and a heron
kept edgy company. Family groups
have taken to the fishing, settling
along both sides of the pond,
their lines laid on calm waters.
Mothers, gifted with an hour's sunshine,
lead a caravan of children along paths
reclaimed recently from sloganeers.
A worked-for tranquillity frames the day.

The Heavy Gang

Lynched by
Winter's heavy gang
Geraniums, lilies, cyclamen
Are now a mangled heap.

Even snowdrops
Pluckier than most
Don't hang about just yet.
They watch their backs.

Only the Lenten rose
Reveals a touch of mauve,
Giving us a hint
Of penance just ahead.

That mini desert crossed
We'll slough off
Thoughts of death
And wait for resurrection.

Scar

The master led us from the classroom,
ranged us round the lime tree - one of a row
that flanked the school - and pointed silently
to a raw gash in its grey bark.

"Now, Liam" He signalled to the boy we knew
as the smart one in our primary class,
who then began...
>   *I think that I shall never see*
>   *a poem lovely as a tree*

continuing in his posh poetry voice
to the line that rang like a funeral bell

>   *But only God can make a tree.*

Some of the lads smirked discreetly.
"Look!" the master then declaimed."Just look
at the damage done to God's creation!"
adding that the guilty boy was in our midst.

I shared the shudder this announcement caused,
then watched, appalled, as his raised finger
turned to point at me. I heard myself gasping
"Me, sir?" my words spilling out in hot denial.

Sympathetic murmurs bolstered my nerve.
"Someone has told you a lie ,sir" And if
he expected a sobbing penitent
he met instead my injured innocence.

No witness was produced, no evidence
supplied: no apology ever made.

Yesterday I passed those limes, school's
sentinels still erect but showing their age.
In time-darkened bark no scar and April airs
setting the young leaves dancing.

Technology

I taught myself to type decades ago,
no single-fingered poking at the keys
but the two-handed skills the key-chart showed.
I progressed fast and pride grew with my speed.
My Hermes Baby's satisfying clatter
pleased me, convinced me of my expertise
as I despatched reports to every quarter.
My Baby travelled everywhere with me.

All that was forty years ago and now
it's this computer stuff. My Microsoft
defies me. Faults occur, I don't know how
for I still exercise my typing craft,
and while I'm ready to explore fresh ground
technology can get a fellow down.

Spring Song

"Write me a page on spring," he said.
We, city lads all, set down
what we believed we knew about
the countryside – the farmer bent
behind the plough, tailed by the gulls,
buds bursting everywhere, primroses
brightening the banks, snowdrops
shyly peeping: but mostly we outdid
ourselves in writing of the lambs
that gambolled o'er the green, certain
we'd caught the season with our pens.

"Look, lads. That's a spring day" he said.
"Take a turn outside. Breathe deeply.
Notice the air. Any new activity?
See what the birds are up to.
Have a look at the trees, the hedges.
What about the hills beyond the school.
Come back then and write that page again."

Greetings

Feliz Ano Novo
the voice was cheery on the phone
six thousand miles away.

Our New Year days still trail
their shawls of rain from late December.

Round the dripping larch magpies swoop,
patrolling the aisles of evening
like warders rattling their keys.

Green arrows break through weathered wood-chip
and wet earth, outriders of the mighty
army massing no more than a month or two away.

I turn from the window and reply
Feliz Ano Novo,
pleased to fancy my winter words
will blossom in distant sun.

Latitudes 1

Three mounted gauchos pass, sombreroed,
tented in thick ponchos that droop
to stirrup level. They ride, bowed
into the wind that rakes the pampas
and against which my long overcoat
makes no defence. Thin shoes drink
mud that hooves have churned.

No comfort promised in homes ahead
for all are heartless, and suddenly
I'm stabbed with longings for nights
back in Belfast round the fire,
butter melting on a plate of toast,
a mug of cocoa in my hand.

Latitudes 2

Worth the short trip from Macapá,
we thought, to stand beside the posts
marking the line and feel equator heat.
It was a stretch of scrubby ground
without trees, so we were exposed,
but the high sun that day
did not lean heavily on us.
Our shadows curled like cats about
our feet. A light wind, coming from
the coast where Amazon took on
the Atlantic, tempered the air.
We felt at ease, took photos
of each other, drove off content
that we had not been bested by the heat
while sampling zero latitude.

A Gift from the Night

The tropical night, wrapping me round,
made the unfamiliar region even more
strange. If there were homes anywhere,
none showed in the blackness.
My headlights threw brightness only
on the uneven road ahead, reflecting
off the sandy stretches unstable
under the wheels, so, when the car spun
I failed to hold it and it leaped
across a low ditch into a field,
the lights stroking through corn stalks.

Miles from anywhere!
I despaired. Now what?
Within minutes came an answer.
Conjured from the sooty darkness,
many figures appeared. Men, boys,
one with a lamp. With cheery reassurance
they had the car back on the road
and me overwhelmed with their kindness.
"Gente fina" one of them remarked
as I gave what I hoped might buy
them all some beer.

Hello, Mossoró

In the greengrocers, Castle Street,
searching through Galia melons
I find a sunripe one and a name
that surprises, sets me remembering.

Well hello there, Mossoró!
I want to wave in friendliness
across a gap of forty years.

Rainy season, North East Brazil,
and I am driving through streams
that bite the red earth of the road
and spit out mud. A journey where
the constant watchfulness wearies
the eye, travelling, morass beset,
to an unknown town. Happy relief, then
that it opens up to me and, in a short while
rings me round with friends

Yes, well I remember Mossoró

Vendors on the Avenida

Beside the pushy lottery sellers
and clamorous newsboys on the Avenida,
he was a silent, ignorable vendor.

Old too; his crumpled suit, stringy tie
and sweat-soiled fedora suggested
his past had been better than his present.

Resting heavily on his arm, pamphlets
detailing government regulations;
meant for sale, they rarely found a buyer.

Once his hunched wretchedness so troubled me
I bought a copy: enough for a bite and sup,
I consoled myself, as he shuffled away.

When I passed his pitch again, there he stood,
a fat cigar clamped in his thin lips,
and on his face a look of utter bliss.

Memory Burr

He staggers and falls beside
a market stall piled with melons,
his white shirt bloodied where he has been
stabbed. Round him a small crowd gathers.

"O sol" he winces, and someone moves
to block its midday glare from him.
Some neighbours raise him, half-drag,
half-carry him towards a shadowed porch.

His thin, cotton trousers begin
to slip – slip until his bare buttocks
are exposed. Someone near me giggles,
- like a knife hacking through the silence.

        * * *

It was a boy, thirteen, fourteen,
his expression mirthless, a look almost
of shock on his face. I remember
hoping the dying man had heard nothing.

Memory has its burrs, and this one
has me wondering if that youth in later years
ever relived that moment. Did it cling
to his mind quite as long as it has to mine?

Water-Lilies

All July the water-lilies thrived
and now their yellow cups extend
across the upper pond, bright as the blobs
of country butter I remember
surfacing in a wooden churn
in Katie Conway's kitchen.
Its taste, salty on our bread but welcome
when rationing determined our supply.

More distant drifts of blooms
bring to mind a phrase – bóthar na mine buí
– road of the yellow meal – built in the Rosses
in famine times when meal
was the wage for killing toil.
But here on the buttery surfaces
– lovely to the eye – nothing feeds
Only the coots make their slow way
through the dense lily pads.

Weeds and Wheels

He doesn't notice that his garden plot
has fallen to the weeds. Now cabbage whites

and meadow-browns have made themselves
at home, sparking the gloom of nettles.

Cuckoo flowers, daisies and buttercups
tussle for dominance, easily

out-manoeuvred by the dandelion clan.
Bindweed, that well known hanger-on,

annexing neighbours for its climb,
can see itself in the gleaming panels

of his new Merc smirking in the sun.
His Sunday worship guarantees that shine,

his labouring a kind of prayer,
the engine's murmur his only hymn.

The weeds, meanwhile, bring to their stolen space
unflagging vigour and a transient grace.

Haymaking

Remembering distant Augusts when, as kids,
we trooped behind old Arthur and his sons
round hayfields at Aughacarnaghan,

watching their skilful knitting of forkfuls
into steady stacks, loving the breaks when,
counted among the men for mugs of tea

and buttered soda farls, we'd stretch our length
on the stubble – we thought it would be fun
cashing those memories for real hay-making

now that John in Dunnyvadden was starting
on his field. In full sun next day, and full heart
we joined the farm-hands following the baler.

It chopped, tied, packed and dropped the glinting bales.
No fork-work but a building up in blocks of six.
The farm lads set a fast pace and our skill

grew slowly with them but so too did the task
as untried muscles learned to cope with pain.
Jag-toothed ends of bales trailed signatures

in blood on our bare arms. The lowering sun
cut like a blade across our eyes. Evening
saw us in the barn, bales stacked to the roof,

a gold stour spreading, filling noses, mouths,
sticking to sweaty skin. A wash, a bite and sup,
we dropped like stones into our beds that night

Next morning early from a nearby field
the groaning baler pummelled me awake
and every fibre in my body squealed.

Josie

The smile, partnering deep brown eyes,
made her a welcome visitor. Her tanned
face gave her a Romany look though
all she ever read were teacups. Never
gave the slightest thought to what she wore
always the tweedy coat and brown beret.

She knew the seed and breed of all
the countryside, which made her chatter
story-rich but not malicious, so
no one's door was closed to her. Advice
she gave on many matters – cures
for stings and rheumy aches and boils.

Recipes for soups and jams and beef-tea;
how to cook eels, take grass stains out of shirts,
even carpets though she owned none herself.
People savoured her tales, smiled, knowing
Josie gave little time to her own housework.
 "Must go" she'd say, heading for the door .

The parting words would see her linger
a while longer and another story surface.
Then, a shake of the shoulders, a smile
and she'd be off, though the road might lead her
to another door, another cup of tea, or,
if the light was fading, propel her home.

Safe House

The Blitz made us evacuees
The house where we were billeted
was small, The owner lived in one room.
Then there was Sean.

He was a kind of guest. Youngish,
yet his chest rasped like an old man's.
Spent time in his room, listening
to the radio. Ate meals there too.

Sometimes he would join us, ask us
about the books we'd read. Wanted
to know if we'd been scared when bombs
were falling. Taught us "battleships".

When he took the air, Sean always
stayed behind the house, never the front.
I saw him reading as he walked –
My Fight for Irish Freedom.

I felt uneasy about it, especially
when I saw him watch from behind
the curtains once as a policeman
cycled past on the road to Toome.

Then, one day his room was empty.
Sean never did return, nor did we
ever ask why he had gone
or where he might be heading.

Freety People

They are wood touchers, wary of the unforeseen;
ash clearers from the hearths of the old year.
First-footers, a dark-haired breed, bearing
the new year into neighbours' houses
with lumps of coal. They sidle past leaning
ladders, deplore the indoor opening
of umbrellas, spilt salt, broken mirrors.
But shooting stars, rainbows, the new moon's
sickle revive in them the possibility
of better things and wishes granted.

An aunt, cheery upholder of all such
fancies, would, on her visits, urge us out
under a spangled sky to count the stars,
seven each night for seven nights, for luck.
She possessed a tiger's whisker, inventing
stories as to how she came upon it.
Big magic; she wore it wrapped round her finger
but only let us rub it gently. We loved
her coming for we knew that, deep
in her capacious handbag, lurked pokes of sweets.

Attaboy

While awaiting the 61 bus
on this clear October morning
there is time to enjoy the sight
of Cavehill in a cloud of brightness
and feel the familiar affection.
I want to run my hand over
its pleasing bulk, saying "attaboy".
A comfort to know that it's always there,

friendly, relaxed like a big dog
at an open fire, not given to barking
or chasing cats, not needing
a leash or a juicy bone.
Some days when it is kennelled
in gloom I imagine I hear it
whimpering but, given a bit
of sun, just see how it glows.

Famine in the Skies

What seemed a fallen flower head,
pale lilac grey, was a small fledgling
dead on the driveway, directly
below the muddy conch housemartins
had in past years plastered to our eaves.

Days of hammering rain had brought
famine to the skies; to nestlings too.
The small bill gaped, unfed.
Frail crumpled wings would never
open over Africa.

A fly-past of martins heading south
let fall a sprinkle of chirrupings.
The chick, its final nest a match-box,
was laid beneath a flowering bush
where birds would sing.

Intruder

The screech from the bathroom
splits the morning peace, proclaims
an alien presence behind the door,
a black intruder whose velocity
on eight legs round the bath tub
deepens the panic.

As the only knight within call
I equip myself for the confrontation
-one small cup, one piece of card.
Eschewing violence I act deaf
to the testy order that I show
no mercy.

A quick scoop with my weapons
and the beast curls up in defeat.
I find an open window and propel
it into the laurel hedge, from whence
no doubt, it will return in time
to spur another hue and cry.

Taking October Slowly

Enough heat still to coax me for a while
to a park bench, to take October
slowly, feeling the colours deserve
a closer, more appreciative look.
"Not a bad oul morning, that" a walker,
passing, cheerily observes.
A windless day of golden light; now
and then, the lisping leaf-fall of lime
and ash and sycamore enhance the stillness.
A slip of cloud on the sky's rim, motionless,
leaves the pale blue to a modest sun.
On the pond, the water-fowl in neutral
gear respect the hour's tranquillity.
No, not a bad day. Not bad at all.

Irrelevant

Aesop sets the scene.
Crow on a high branch,
a lump of cheese in her bill.
Covetous fox below, about
to exercise his wiles —
how to transfer the morsel
from bill to open jaws.

The lesson of the fable weighed
lightly on my eight years.
But I did wonder – why cheese?
Why not just a hunk of bread?
Decades passed before I learned
that birds find cheese most palatable.
Foxes too.
Which leads me now to speculate
about lacunae in my education brought
on by my penchant for irrelevancy

Rough Crossing

The ferry from Fishguard rounded
Strumble Head and took broadside
the first green rollers.
Howls, some in mock dismay,
arose from the passengers.
"Daddy, daddy!" squealed a small boy.
"Don't be tiresome darling. You know
daddy and I are divorced" Her hand
rested on the thigh of her new man
who smiled. "I'm daddy now".
The other children looked away.
The ship, heading west to Rosslare,
pitched cruelly in another wave.
Moans now mingled with shouts
and above the clamour the sound
of the weepy child being tiresome again.
No guarantee of anything ahead.
A rough crossing from shore to shore.

Shots

The grocery van reverses over
a plastic bottle at the kerb.
The sharp report sweeps pigeons
from the roofs and throws them
in a swirl of panic overhead.

Thirty years or so ago another
pigeon generation roosting on
the school chimney stack
signalled alarm in the same
wild loops above Ardoyne.

Was that a shot? we used to ask,
watching them rise, though it
could have been a slammed door
or a back-fire. The birds had no answer.
They rose, taking no chances.

Dodecahedron

A TV quiz show sprang the word
on players, stirred an old memory.
Later that night I plucked from dusty
exile on a shelf my own
neglected dodecahedron.
Not that I loved it but it brought
to mind a distant course pursued
when New Mathematics was the thing,
meant to yank me and many others
from old ways of teaching towards modernity.
Not to have sought the "New" might well
have left me fossilised, chalk-fingered,
blackboard-bound. But what alone
survives is this twelve-sided solid,
each face a pentagon, a gesture,
towards some bright ideas that
all too quickly lost their shine.

Value for Money

Christopher's usually mischievous look
gave way to one of excitement.
"Sir, that book was brill " he said

"I'd give you a pound for it."
Christopher, keen reader? Christopher
offering good money for a book?

And the book? *Little Mrs Pepperpot*.
Well, well. An historic first. No one
had ever made such an offer before.

Then, on Monday, one pound appeared.
The deal was real. I said I'd try to find
another *Pepperpot*. "You've read that one"

And in town, I did; price fifty p.
A new book and at a discount.
His grin was uncontainable.

Preparing for Secondary, now eleven,
Christopher found me in my room,
patted my hand, dropped on my desk,

the worse for wear *Mrs P.*
"Put that in the class library, sir"
Flashed me a smile of benefaction .

Easy Pleasing

It was easy in those days to please them;
a big bottle of brightly coloured sweets,
enough to give every boy a handful on the day
before the school's Christmas break.

As a tradition it retained its charm,
remained a treat for years.
Pocket money, a slim resource;
teacher-given sweets seemed sweeter.

The day the world changed was when
the boys started throwing sweets
they didn't like into the bin. The report,
as sweet hit metal, went through me.

Sweets you don't like? Unbelievable!
You've *got* to like sweets! Pleasure
is what they are made to give.
I told them how it was in my young days.

A ha'penny a week didn't stretch far,
but it bought four caramels, sometimes
five, depending on the shop. It meant
a furious session of bargain hunting.

They laughed at that of course. A different
generation; inflated expectations, but still,
great kids. I hope these scary times
have not undone their hopes.

School Outing

It was the P5's day for Crawfordsburn,
sun guaranteed. The minibus along
the bypass paralleled the railway line
as an accordeon of voices hailed
the train's passing with a lively chorus –
Down by the dandelion field
watching the holiday trains go by
all afternoon we waited, Billy and I –

The poem fragment, newly learned, was hoisted
like a banner carolling their joy each time
a loco hustled by, and each mile passed.

Less a crocodile, more like twentyfive
young greyhounds on one leash, until they reached
the beach, then clamour and a scattering.
The waiting waters leaped to meet their squeals.

Along the shore rock pools were shaded by
the looming shapes of boys, voices crackling
excitedly, each "Sir, sir!" signalling
discoveries. Safari ceased when

Fantas, Cokes and sandwiches appeared.
"Don't leave a pick of rubbish, do you hear!"
Pockets that held sweets made room for shells
and pebbles and the carcasses of crabs.

Marty's First Communion coat got stained
Dee lost his tee shirt to the waves, Sean ripped
his jeans, Steve gathered sea-pinks for his gran
and everybody got a touch of sun.

Less vigour on the bus but still they found
voice to make the wonder last
till that train was out of sight
we waved, Billy and I did,
we waved with all our might

Then, in a slow unwinding of the spell,
they shuffled home trailing a seashore smell.

All the Hands

"Nobody likes me, sir", he said
standing at my desk. I suspected
it was true, but denied it.
"Nonsense, Seanie, don't I like you?"

Next day, school outing. He'd come
empty-handed, his shirt flying,
not a button left on it.
No togs, no gear, no lunch.

"Seanie has no lunch. Who can help?"
Up shot the hands. More than half the class.
Mars bars, Kit Kats, Chews, Coke,
landed on his desk.

A wholly happy day by the sea. Afterwards,
"Well, Seanie, what do you remember most?"
"All the hands sir," he said
Yes Seanie, all the hands.

The Eleven Plus

" Well boys?" We'd ask as they streamed
from the classroom where the exam
was staged. "Wee buns!" they'd reply
and hurry past. It was the cool response
of the less-than-interested, for it was
just another knot encountered
in the thick plank of their schooling.

The more serious dispensed with
the nonchalance, gave a measured response.
But by and large, each, in time, honed
his own blade, sawed through timber
as it came, hoping for an easy grain.

Still that Face

She is some way behind the other
family members moving slowly
down the aisle behind the coffin
but he knows that face at once,
its gentle oval still unsettling
though criss-crossed now by
the lane-ways of half a century.

He feels a tightening in
his throat as he sees her need
of a neighbour's supporting arm.
She turns her head as if looking
for faces. He hopes her eyes
don't light on the old man hiding
his sorrow in the shadows.

The Lights Gone Dead

When a string of fairy lights went dead
I knew replacements were imperative
to match the sparkle neighbours' homes displayed.
But shop after shop sold out left me surprised.
Woolies just might have something left to please.
"Sorry luv" the shop girl said "All gone."
Gone too my fancy - future Christmas trees
decked in the last lights of a famous store.
I felt commercial winter in the aisles,
a sense of walking on a tilting deck.
Redundancy beset the shop girls' smiles.
No saviour coming, no one with the knack.
Wondered if, on the bleak day to come,
they'd sound retreat on a sixpenny drum.

Praise Him

When snowdrop candles temper the searing
frost we glimpse him, will him to be near.
In April's alleluias of warblings,
of wings and breaking buds we know he's here.
In summer's carnival, most clearly seen
among climbing bells, delphinium towers,
geraniums and roses velvet rioting,
the mute cacophony of humbler flowers.
We find him through seasons' certainties
in turning, burning leaves and berries' fire,
the pity and the beauty of the naked trees,
the violence of clouds, the crumbling skies.
For him no vision of an underclass.
Find him in creeping weed and trampled grass.

Winter-Flowering Cherry

Best encountered unexpectedly
in a corner of half shadows
or against an old wall
where pale light filters down;
to be touched, to wonder
how those small blossoms,
frail, reticent, can so generously
veil the branches, lend them
an off-white glimmer almost
like a web on a still morning,
so insubstantial that a snap
of wind might tear them down.
But the tree stands steadfast;
the grace of February
year after year.